SOUTHERN EMUs SINCE PF

in Colour

For the Modeller and His...

Bruce Oliver

Ian Allan
PUBLISHING

First published 2011

ISBN 978 0 7110 3627 7

© Bruce Oliver 2011

Published by Ian Allan Publishing

an imprint of Ian Allan Publishing Ltd,
Hersham, Surrey, KT12 4RG
Printed in England by Ian Allan Printing Ltd,
Hersham, Surrey, KT12 4RG

Code: 1112/A1

Distributed in the United States of America and
Canada by BookMasters Distribution Services

Visit the Ian Allan Publishing website at
www.ianallanpublishing.com

Title page:
New Milton May 2010
The station buildings date from the line's
opening in 1888, on the later direct route to
Bournemouth. The station is visibly well
maintained. In this scene, the station hosts
Class 444 No 444014 on a service from
Waterloo to Poole.

CONTENTS

INTRODUCTION

This book and its immediate predecessor, *Southern EMUs before Privatisation in Colour*, combine to form a sequel to the original publication, *Southern Region Electrics in Colour*. As with the two preceeding publications, all pictures are from the same portfolio and all were taken by the author. The choice of pictures has been determined by the competing demands of rolling stock and location. It is therefore hoped an acceptable balance may have been struck, satisfying the need to embrace many different classes of unit and a wide variety of liveries, while featuring a significant numbert of different stations and locations denied inclusion in the two previous books.

Bibliography
A Regional History of the Railways of Great Britain, Volumes 2 (Southern England and *3 (Greater London),* H. P. White, David & Charles.
History of the Southern Railway, C. F. Dendy Marshall (revised by R. W. Kidner), Ian Allan.
PLS Field Guide, Railways of the Southern Region, Geoffrey Body, Patrick Stephens.
Railway Track Diagrams — Southern and TFL, TRACK Maps.

Left:
St. Denys November 1999
Connex-liveried Phase II '4CIG' No 1860 leaves the 1866 line from Netley, to join the main line from Waterloo. The train, bound for Bournemouth, has come from Victoria. The station opened in 1861. Although the main line was electrified in 1967, the connection to the junctions at Port Creek and Farlington had to wait a further 23 years for the 3rd rail.

South Eastern

The franchise was awarded to Connex, to run from 14 October 1996 until 9 November 2003, with the possibility of an extension to 2011. Somewhat prematurely, circumstances arose that necessitated the Strategic Rail Authority taking over the operation, with the franchise rescinded on 26 June 2003. The SRA formed its own subsidiary company, South East Trains, with Connex granted a six-month stay of execution until finally relinquishing control. While this might appear to have been a case of renationalisation, it was in effect no more than a holding operation until the franchise was re-let to Govia in November 2005, with an eight-year agreement starting on 1 April 2006. The branding of the operation became Southeastern, using a white livery with yellow doors. This replaced the Connex scheme of white and yellow, with script in blue; an additional blue strip was later included on 'Networker' body sides.

For main-line services, Connex inherited a fleet of Mk I rolling stock comprising '4CEP' and '4VEP' units, with a few '4CIG' units infiltrating later. Eighteen '4CEP' units were eventually reduced to three-coach formations (Nos 1101-18), offering enhanced power/weight and acceleration. In 1994-95 there had arrived 16 Class 365 'Networker Express' units (Nos 365501-16) but, with the arrival of Class 375 'Electrostars', the Class 365 units were transferred to join First Capital Connect units (Nos 365517-541), for services out of King's Cross. Class 375 'Electrostar' units were delivered in five batches between 1999 and 2004, comprising three-coach units Nos 375301-310 and four-coach units Nos 375601-630/701-715/801-830/901-927. Nos 375901-927 differ from earlier batches inasmuch as they offer only suburban-type 3+2 seating in Standard Class. Five-coach inner-suburban Class 376 'Electrostars' (Nos 376001-036) were delivered in 2004-05, gangwayed within units only but with 2+2, rather than 3+2, Standard Class seating throughout. More recently, six-coach Class 395 units (Nos 395001-029) were delivered for HS1 express services from east Kent to St Pancras, the timetable commencing in December 2009. These units are equipped to operate in both 750V DC third rail and 25kV AC mode.

Privatised suburban services inherited 'Networker' Classes 465 and 466 from Network SouthEast. Class 465 had been built in three batches between 1991 and 1994, Nos 465001-050, 465151-197 (BREL/ABB) and 465201-250 (Metro-Cammell). Two-coach Class 466 'Networkers' Nos 466001-043 (GEC-Alstom) joined the four-coach squadrons in 1994-95. In 2005 units Nos 465201-234 were refurbished at Doncaster, when 1st Class accommodation was incorporated in order that they might be employed on outer-suburban and coastal services; they were renumbered 465901-934. Earlier all 'Networkers' had been end-modified by the addition of curved covers over the cab corner steps, to deter intending 'surfers'.

In 1998 12 Class 508 units, then surplus to requirements on the Mersey electrified lines, were taken out of storage and refurbished at Eastleigh for use by Connex, being renumbered 508201-212. Deployed mainly on Medway Valley services and the Sittingbourne to Sheerness-on-Sea branch, they also found employment on through services between London Bridge and Tunbridge Wells via Redhill. Earlier they had been used on services that linked Kent with Gatwick. They were taken out of service in December 2008, when Southern took over operation of the route linking Redhill with Tonbridge.

South Central

Connex had been awarded the South Central franchise six months earlier than that for South Eastern. Initially the franchise was to run from 12 April 1996 for 15 years, but this was revised on 17 July 1998 to be subject to reissue in 2003. In the event, the operation was not distinguished by success and, as with Connex South Eastern, the franchise was rescinded, taking effect on 24 October 2000, 2½ years early. Financial arrangements, dated 15 June 2001, laid the foundations for Govia to acquire share capital in Connex South Central. Thus, Govia became the franchisee-in-waiting during the interim period up to May 2003, from which point it assumed control with a six-year agreement due to expire on 20 September 2009. In June 2009 Govia was successful in retaining the franchise for a further six years, with an extension to eight years conditional upon performance. Govia is owned jointly by the Go-Ahead group and Keolis. The marketing title 'South Central' disappeared officially on 30 May 2004,

when the brand name 'Southern' was exhumed from the distant past, under which attractive banner the operator has since become recognised. Historically, Connex must be credited with initiating services across London to Rugby, as well as introducing through services between Victoria and Bournemouth, though this latter operation was later curtailed to turn back at Southampton. For the purpose of route knowledge, the Southern timetable allows for the line via Botley and Eastleigh to Southampton to be used.

As in the case of South Eastern, Connex South Central inherited a large portfolio of Mk I main-line rolling stock (Phases I and II '4CIG' and '4BIG' units, together with '4VEP' units), with some units receiving a version of the new Southern colour scheme. In 1997-98 Connex created a sub-class of Phase II '4CIG' stock, when 11 units were reduced to three-coach formations, as '3COP' Nos 1401-11, with the former 1st Class 'opened out' for Standard use on Coastway services. (Just prior to withdrawal, several surviving units were restored to four-coach formations.) For suburban operations, Connex took on 46 units of four-coach Class 455s (Nos 801-846), all 24 units of two-coach Class 456s (Nos 001-024), and 20 units of Class 319s (Nos 001-013/214-220). All units in Classes 455 and 456 were subsequently refurbished, with those in Class 455 losing their outer gangway connections. 'Electrostar' rolling stock dates from 2001/02, prior to Govia assuming total command, when three-coach Class 375/3 Nos 375311-338 arrived. These units were later renumbered 377301-328, following replacement of Tightlock couplings by Dellner.

By the time Mk I stock was finally eliminated from the system on 26 November 2005, Southern had acquired, apart from the 28 three-coach 'Electrostars' (see above), 154 four-coach 'Electrostars' (Nos 377101-164/201-215/401-475). The 3772xx batch was equipped, as built, for dual-voltage operation, for services via North Pole Junction to points on the West Coast Main Line — Watford Junction initially, but more recently Milton Keynes. Class 319s (qv) had operated Connex services to Rugby from June 1997 until May 2002, when the service was curtailed at Watford Junction. Class 377/3 units, meanwhile, have been used principally on Coastway services and fast Victoria-Brighton diagrams, where flexibility allows for rakes of three, six, nine and 12 coaches.

Whereas Nos 377301-328 (formerly 375311-338) and 377101-119 were delivered with 2+2 seating throughout Standard Class, later arrivals were equipped with both 2+2 and 3+2 high-density (suburban-type) seating. Deliveries from No 377140 onwards have 3+2 seating in internal vehicles only, the outer driving vehicles retaining 2+2 in Standard Class, with tables and armrests (the 1st Class sections are distinguishable only by antimacassars). A further distinguishing feature is the choice of upholstery. Deliveries to Connex specification were outshopped in the same quality of material as that used in the Class 375 on Southeastern, but later deliveries (the overwhelming majority, to Southern specification) received a coarser turquoise fabric, harder-wearing perhaps but arguably less attractive. Externally, all units carry a colour scheme incorporating white, light green and dark green, with semi-circular features at vehicle ends. The driving vehicle ends are in light green with standard yellow panels. Class 377/4 was delivered in two batches, for main-line work as well as for outer-suburban work, and for the Oxted line, which is now regarded as outer-suburban. These units replaced the last Mk I survivors in passenger service and are interchangeable with Class 377/1, some of which class were designated for suburban use and allocated to Selhurst Depot (SU).

The Class 319 units inherited by Connex South Central formed part of a complicated class history, upgrading, downgrading and livery changes affecting the entire fleet, in association with the Thameslink project. When built, Class 319/1 differed from Class 319/0 inasmuch as it offered 1st Class accommodation. At privatisation, Connex South Central acquired those members of Class 319/0 that had already been transferred from the Thameslink project to the Central Division, solely for use on south London suburban services; a plan to isolate 25kV overhead equipment in these units was later abandoned, with the prospect of further use north of the Thames. Some of these Class 319/0 units were subsequently fitted with 1st Class accommodation, arranged as a lounge bar, after becoming Nos 319214-220. For a while, units thus converted operated the 'Connex Express' from 27 January 1997, a London-Brighton service omitting a Gatwick stop, becoming 12-coach formations during 'rush hour' periods. More recently, Southern-operated Nos 319001-013/214-220 were transferred, in stages, to First Capital Connect, the successor to Thameslink (qv). Prior to this

final transfer, Southern units could be found operating between Bedford and points south of the Thames, when units were borrowed to augment First Capital Connect services. Since the Class 319 transfer, Class 377s have operated some suburban services. Of historical note, Class 319 Nos 319008/009 operated the first passenger-carrying train through the Channel Tunnel, being named *Cheriton* and *Coquelles* respectively, in recognition.

With the renewal of the South West Trains franchise in 2006 came the abandonment of that company's through services to Brighton. As a direct consequence, Southern extended its grip on services to the west, with Havant receiving more Southern services per hour than SWT – three to/from Portsmouth serving Littlehampton, Brighton and Victoria and two to/from Southampton serving Brighton and Victoria. With this revision, trains to/from Victoria coupled and uncoupled at Horsham, instead of at Barnham, with only the Bognor sections calling at intermediate stations between Barnham and Horsham. Southampton services had previously coupled and uncoupled at Haywards Heath, in association with the Eastbourne operation.

With the renewed Stagecoach franchise for SWT came a surprising development, the disposal of Class 442 from February 2007. For about two years the 24 units remained stored out of use at Eastleigh. Happily, they were to be rescued by Southern, taking advantage of SWT's decision to dispose. Thus, by the summer of 2009 all 24 units had been acquired for operation by Southern, albeit not all in service. A programme of refurbishment at Wolverton was put in hand, the units emerging branded Gatwick Express for use on both Gatwick services and peak-period operations between Victoria and Brighton, as well as Eastbourne.

Most recently a batch of 19 Class 313s (313201-217/219/220) found new employment with Southern, following their displacement by Class 378s on London Overground services.

Gatwick Express

The franchise for the dedicated services between Gatwick Airport and Victoria, Gatwick Express, was awarded to National Express, initially as a 15-year agreement starting on 28 April 1996. Rolling stock comprised a squadron of 14 Class 73 electro-diesel locomotives (Nos 73201-13/235, to be found coupled at the country end), ten Class 489 DMLVs (Nos 489101-

110, coupled at the London end), and two batches of Mk II trailer sets (two-coach Nos 488201-210 and three-coach Nos 488302-319), assembled in rakes as dictated by demand. In 1999-2000 eight new purpose-built eight-coach units, Class 460 Nos 460001-008, delivered by Alstom, replaced inherited stock. From time to time advertising liveries were carried by Class 460, as had been the case with the Class 488 trailer sets. Things were to change dramatically, however, leading up to Southern's renewed franchise in 2009. The Gatwick Express operation was absorbed by Southern, with Class 460 Gatwick Express rolling stock joined by Class 442, a move imposed, inappropriately, by the Department of Transport, as Class 442 had not been designed for this type of operation. That the Class 460 units should be transferred away from the route for which they were specifically designed suggests decisions being taken by people who do not understand railway operation.

Thameslink and First Capital Connect

The project opened for custom in the summer of 1988, with subsequent service revision. Under privatisation, an initial seven-year franchise was let to Govia on 30 January 1997, with services starting on 2 March 1997. The franchise was subsequently let to First Capital Connect, running from 1 April 2006 to 31 March 2015. Initially, Bedford, Luton and Cricklewood were variously connected with Gatwick, Brighton, Sevenoaks and a collection of intermediate stations. There was also the Wimbledon 'circular', taking Class 319s through Tooting, St Helier and Sutton. Guildford had entered the frame in 1991 but, as with Sevenoaks, the link did not last. Initially Class 319 comprised two sub-classes, Nos 319001-060 (without 1st Class) and 319161-186 (with 1st Class). Nos 319001-020 (with Nos 319014-020 later becoming 319214-220) were, as recorded above, transferred to the Central Division for use on services south of London. Units Nos 319021-060 were later upgraded, with the provision of 1st Class accommodation, becoming Nos 319421-460 for use on 'City Flyer' services between Bedford and Brighton. Meanwhile, units Nos 319161-186 lost their 1st Class accommodation, becoming Nos 319361-386, initially for 'City Metro' services. More recently, all Class 319 units remaining with Southern passed to First Capital Connect, by which time deliveries of Class 377/5 'Electrostars' had commenced, with the original Thameslink project due for further expansion. Sevenoaks returned to the timetable in the summer of 2009, while infiltration to other destinations in Kent was set in motion, with Gillingham and Ashford in the frame.

The range of liveries applied to Class 319 since privatisation has produced an astonishing variety of schemes, almost sufficient to provide material for a book in itself. Variations to be found within specific schemes might indeed be said to confound. Advertising liveries, combined with a seemingly ever-changing programme of detail changes within a corporate identity, have provided a bewildering source of material. Often variations have been very short-lived, while in many cases individual units have been the only carriers of the scheme displayed. It will therefore not be the purpose of this book to dwell disproportionately upon the class, given the need to perform a balancing act among the many contenders for inclusion throughout the system, not least of which is the wealth of station settings, emphasising the importance of context.

South West Trains

The franchise for South West Trains (SWT), a seven-year lease won by Stagecoach, dated from 6 February 1996; a three-year deal in July 2003 extended the franchise to 4 February 2007. During 2006 Stagecoach was successful in renewing the franchise, this time for a ten-year lease, to last until 2017. Complications such as those affecting both Connex franchises were not to affect SWT. Nevertheless, under the renewed franchise in 2006 the company perhaps exercised financial brinkmanship in substantially outbidding its nearest rival to gain the Department of Transport's hand. The funds required to fulfil the Department's conditions of operation were then to place a heavy burden of responsibility not only upon the company but also upon passengers, as the source of income. Economies duly followed, predicated by the demands of the agreement.

In 1996 SWT took over a substantial operation, one that extended far beyond the electrified system, with Class 159 diesel services to Exeter, later to serve Bristol, Paignton, Plymouth and Penzance. In the inner-suburban area 98 four-coach Class 455 units (Nos 455701-50/847-74/901-20) provided the foundation of the service structure. All Class 455 units were later repainted and refurbished, with 2+2 suburban seating and increased standing

area. Main-line services were originally in the hands of four-coach units from Classes 412 ('4BEP'), 421 ('4CIG') and 423 ('4VEP'), with flagship rolling stock comprising the 24 five-coach Class 442 ('Wessex') units. During the early stages of privatisation, representatives of Class 411 ('4CEP') appeared in increasing numbers, refugees from South Eastern Division services; these were units that had inaugurated the electrification schemes in Kent during 1959 and 1961/62. During the early 1980s mid-term refurbishment of '4CEP' and '4BEP' stock at Swindon had resulted in the complete rebuilding of vehicles within their original body shells.

Class 442 had been designed specifically for Bournemouth and Weymouth services, its introduction in 1988 planned to coincide with the extension of electrification to Weymouth. These Mk III units employed electrical equipment recovered from the 1967 Class '4REP' tractor units. It was the '4REP' units, in combination with '4TC' sets, that had inaugurated the push-pull Bournemouth electrification operation. In the early 1990s Network SouthEast decided that the Bournemouth line should share Class 442 with the Portsmouth Direct line. The consequent quid pro quo required certain Bournemouth line services to receive combinations of '4CIG' and '4BEP' stock. The arrangement settled down easily, with Portsmouth-line passengers benefiting from the enhanced status that Mk III rolling stock represented. The arrangement survived well into privatisation, until SWT decided to remove Class 442 from the Portsmouth Direct line early in the new century.

It should be noted that '4VEP' rolling stock was not used exclusively on stopping services, the purpose for which it had been designed, given the generous provision of doors. Twelve-coach rakes of '4VEP' stock could be found on main-line fast and semi-fast schedules, particularly during peak periods – as with both Connex operations (South East and South Central). Combinations of '4VEP', '4CIG', '4CEP' and '4BEP' rolling stock were quite normal, operating at all levels, from stopping trains to main-line express services. As an historical reminder – following Bournemouth's 1967 electrification, where '4REP'/'4TC' combinations worked all fast and semi-fast services – the Portsmouth Direct line had been similarly regimented in 1970, with fast and semi-fast services diagrammed strictly for brand-new 12-coach rakes of '4CIG'/'4BIG'/'4CIG' rolling stock. Twenty-two '4CIG' units (renumbered 1301-22), together with the seven

refurbished '4BEP' units (Nos 2301-07), were modified in the 1980s to achieve enhanced performance, and were designated 'Greyhound' units. Later still, further 'Greyhound' units (Nos 1392-99) were created when eight former '4BIG' units were upgraded, their buffet car vehicles replaced by non-buffet trailer vehicles from '4CEP' units. Finally, the '4BEP' units (Nos 2301-07) exchanged their buffet vehicles with '4CEP' trailers, to provide more accommodation in 'Greyhound' rolling stock. Thus units Nos 2311-17 were created, the plundered '4CEPs' becoming Nos 2321-27, the repository for the downgraded buffet vehicles.

Stagecoach's first delivery of new rolling stock dated from 1998-2000, when 30 Class 458 four-coach gangwayed suburban units (Nos 458001-030) gradually entered service on the Windsor lines out of Waterloo, serving Reading, Weybridge and Guildford via Ascot. These units proved troublesome, seemingly from the start, with various problems coming to light to frustrate the operating department. Further orders were not placed with Alstom. Leading up to the franchise renewal in 2006, almost the entire class had been taken out of service, with units to be found stored at Clapham, Wimbledon and Bournemouth. A complication with the class to attract media exposure concerned the dot-matrix internal display, which, it was claimed, did not meet minimum requirements. With the new franchise came a requirement to reinstate the class and, following modifications and trials, the units have subsequently given an improved return upon investment, generally operating services between Waterloo and Reading.

Following its experience with Class 458, Stagecoach opted for Siemens 'Desiro' rolling stock for the major investment programme to replace its ageing Mk I inheritance. In all, three orders were placed, comprising 45 five-coach Class 444 express units (Nos 444001-045), delivered into service in 2004, and two batches of four-coach Class 450 suburban units (Nos 450001-110/111-127); the first 110 units (Nos 450001-110) were delivered in 2002-03, with 17 further units (Nos 450111-127) entering service mainly during 2006. When the franchise came up for renewal in 2006, decisions were taken that were seriously to affect the balance of rolling stock.

It had been rumoured, in the months leading up to franchise renewal, that Class 458 might be dispatched off-lease as new Class 450 units were by this time operating satisfactorily on Reading services. In the event, Class 458 was reinstated, while

Class 442, very much the flagship of SWT services, was culled. In terms of numbers, it was a zero-sum effect, with 120 Class 442 vehicles taken out of service and 120 Class 458 vehicles reinstated. However, the knock-on effect in terms of public service was to prove unsatisfactory.

SWT had, prior to franchise renewal, operated highly satisfactory express services on both electrified main-line routes. Services had been distinguished by the use of quality rolling stock, guaranteeing passenger comfort and a most agreeable ambience. In 2004 Class 444 replaced Mk I rolling stock on virtually all Portsmouth services, celebrated at the time as 'Portsmouth's New Trains'. All was to change at the beginning of 2007, when the reinstatement of Class 458 precipitated a cascade that bore no detectable relation to public need. Prior to the changes, SWT had operated 69 five-coach main-line express units, comprising 24 Class 442s and 45 Class 444s. With the changes, the number of main-line express units was abruptly reduced by 35% to 45 units, with Class 442 dumped ignominiously on land at Eastleigh Works. SWT was thus no longer able to operate a full high-quality main-line express service on both main lines, with passengers subsequently required to travel in suburban-style units (Class 450) at a level of service for which this class of rolling stock had been neither designed nor deemed appropriate by the builders, Siemens, in the original specification.

In the cascade, Class 444 was largely redeployed to fill the diagrams vacated by Class 442. As a consequence, about half of Portsmouth's weekday main-line express services – together with all Saturday services – were downgraded to Class 450 suburban-style rolling stock, a cascade resulting from changes on the Reading route, where Class 458 had been reinstated. An ultimate irony, consequent upon the cascade, was SWT's unattractive integration of different service levels, requiring Class 444 units to operate stopping services, scarcely the manufacturer's intention for them. The situation resulting from the 2006 franchise was thus unsatisfactory, with Class 442 declared unfit for use for seemingly spurious reasons. That all 24 units were subsequently refurbished for use by Southern on Gatwick and Brighton main-line services (inappropriately but at the Department of Transport's behest) undermined SWT's stated case against Class 442. Logically, Class 442 belongs in SWT front-line service, for which it was designed, with Classes 444 and 450 operating Portsmouth and Reading services respectively. Similarly, Class 460 belongs in Gatwick service, for which it was designed; better, perhaps, had its Alstom bedfellow Class 458 been redeployed with Southern, in the interests of operational convenience.

Left:

Class 375/3: Faversham June 2009
No 375309 departs from platform 3, en route to Dover Priory. This will have been the trailing unit from Victoria, the leading unit having been detached and already on its way to Ramsgate. Station buildings, platforms and canopies are of generous construction and have survived the test of time with distinction. The three-coach Class 375/3 sub-class numbers ten units, Nos 375301-310.

Above:

Class 375/3: Barnham July 2003
No 375315 arrives on a stopping service from Brighton to Portsmouth Harbour. The 28 three-coach Class 375/3 units allocated to South Central/Southern were reclassified as Class 377/3, after modification (Dellner replacing Tightlock couplings). Nos 375311-338 followed the Southeastern batch (Nos 375301-310) numerically but were renumbered 377301-328, 375315 becoming 377305.

Below:

Class 375/6: Ramsgate September 2002
The approach to Ramsgate from Margate dates from early Southern Railway days, when the entire area was redesigned to form the commendably efficient arrangement that exists today. SER Ramsgate Town, on the sea side of the present station, was superseded by the present station, while the LCDR line to Ramsgate Harbour was replaced by a connection, via Dumpton Park, to the new Southern Railway station. The connection opened in 1926. In this view, Class 375/6 No 375612, in its original Connex livery, is about to terminate in Platform 3, heading an eight-coach train from Victoria via Chatham. This sub-class comprises 30 four-coach units, Nos 375601-630.

Above left:

Class 375/7: Folkestone Central August 2009
No 375704 arrives from Charing Cross at the down island platform, during a period when the station served as a temporary terminus, while the line through the Warren to Dover was closed for extensive engineering work. Both down and up services use this island platform, the up island platform lying derelict. There are only fifteen four-coach units in this sub-class, Nos 375701-715.

Centre left:

Class 375/8: Ashford May 2007
No. 375822 is waiting in Platform 6, the outer face of the domestic island which replaced that now dedicated to Eurostar. The high-speed line (HS1) viaduct bypasses the station and is seen to the left. Class 375/8 comprises 30 four-coach units, Nos 375801-830.

Left:

Class 375/9: Tonbridge December 2008
No 375908 stands in Platform 2 with a service to Charing Cross from Ashford and beyond. Officially classified as 'outer suburban' rolling stock, given the use of 3+2 Standard class seating, the units are to be found inter-working with the four other sub-groups of Class 375. There are 27 four-coach units in this sub-class, Nos 375901-927.

Above:

Class 376: Hither Green May 2011
No 376012 displays its clean lines, as it departs Platform 4 for Orpington. The class was delivered into service during 2004-2005, eventually totalling 36 five-coach units, Nos 376001-036.

Below:

Class 377/1: Fratton July 2003
No 377110 leaves Platform 2 on a service from Victoria to Portsmouth Harbour. The unit carries the fresh appearance of one quite recently delivered. This four-coach sub-class runs to 64 units, Nos 377101-164. Seating arrangements are revised in No 377120 onwards, to provide a mix of 3+2 suburban and 2+2 express accommodation.

Left:
Class 377/2: Cosham Junction April 2011
No 377215 uses the west side of the triangle, running from Southampton to Victoria via Portsmouth & Southsea during a period of engineering occupation. The sub-class is equipped to operate in either 750V DC or 25kVAC mode, changing current collection between Shepherd's Bush and North Pole Junction when operating services to and from the LNWR main line. This four-coach sub-class contains 15 units, Nos 377201-215. Inter-regional services operated to Milton Keynes at the time of writing.

Centre left:
Class 377/3: East Croydon March 2010
No. 377313 leads another two members of its sub-class on a nine-coach service to Brighton from Victoria. This unit had entered service as Class 375/3 No 375323, following the Southeastern batch. The sub-class of 28 three-coach units, 377301-328, was renumbered from 375311-338 when Dellner couplings replaced Tightlock.

Bottom left:
Class 377/4: Worthing July 2007
No 377417 is about to depart for Brighton, having come from Littlehampton. The distinctive canopies and valance are of interest, of particular note being the stepped trimming. At the west end of the down platform, ironwork incorporates the Star of David as an artistic device, images of which are also to be found at stations in the north east, such as Scarborough, Middlesbrough and Morpeth. Class 377/4 is the largest sub-class, comprising 75 four-coach units, Nos 377401-475.

Top right:
Class 377/5: Haywards Heath June 2010
No. 377511 arrives in Platform 2 on a service to Brighton from Bedford. The unit is not in 'as delivered' condition, having, by this time, received its First Capital Connect body side vinyls. Comparing this with the picture of No 377522 at East Croydon, seen in 'as delivered' style, the vinyls are, perhaps, a most regrettable, fussy addition to an otherwise clean and dignified livery. Class 377/5 comprises 23 four-coach units, Nos 377501-523.

Right:
Class 378: Clapham Junction September 2009
No 378007 waits in Platform 2, bound for Willesden Junction. These units began to appear in public service from July 2009. The seating arrangement established a complete break with tradition, following the longitudinal pattern of tube stock. Clapham Junction station is a vast complex, comprising 17 platforms in all, though platform 1 is presently out of use. The LSWR arrived on the scene in 1838, the LBSCR and GWR following in 1858 and 1863, respectively. The station was subject to an extensive programme of rebuilding between 1904 and 1907. Class 378 runs to 54 units. Nos 378001-024, delivered as three-coach units, later augmented to four-coach (as 378201-224), are equipped for both 25kV AC and 750V DC operation. Nos 378135-154 were delivered as four-coach units, equipped for 750V DC only. A final batch of four-coach dual-voltage units, Nos 378225-234, has also been delivered.

Top left:

Class 395: Teynham June 2009

No 395010 cruises through the down platform on a training run, prior to introduction of a full timetable of services from east Kent to St.Pancras, via the 25kV High Speed line, west of Gravesend. The class comprises 29 six-coach units, Nos 395001-029.

Bottom left:

Class 444: Redbridge Junction February 2009

No 444040 crosses the junction, en route from Bournemouth to Waterloo. Class 444 comprises 45 five-coach units, Nos 444001-045.

Above:

Class 450: South of Buriton May 2009

No 450084 leads an eight-coach formation on a stopping service from Waterloo to Portsmouth Harbour, here seen just after its descent from Buriton tunnel, a tortuous 1-in-80 path. The class comprises two four-coach batches, Nos 450001-110 and 450111-127. 28 units from the first batch, Nos 450043-070, are reformed as 'High Capacity' units, renumbered 450543-570 (Class 450/5).

Below:

Class 450/5: Chiswick September 2009

No 450545, one of a batch of 28 four-coach units without 1st class accommodation, arrives at the station on a service to Waterloo from Windsor and Eton Riverside. The letters 'HC' refer to 'High Capacity' in respect of available standing room. The station building is one of noted distinction, having the ambience of a fine Victorian urban villa. The station canopy on the up side is of tidy design, with fretwork valance. The station opened in 1849. Down side structures are modern and of minimal appointment but, thankfully, do not distract attention from the architectural gem offered on the other side. Nos 450043-070 were the 28 original units later reformed as Nos 450543-570.

Right:
Class 458: Reading December 2009
No 458006 arrives in Platform 4a, on a service from Waterloo. Trains from Waterloo share Platforms 4a and 4b with First Great Western services from the Guildford direction and Gatwick Airport. Originally, the Southern Railway managed its own station at Reading, on the site presently occupied by the tall buildings seen to the right. Class 458 comprises 30 four-coach units, Nos 458001-030. In the distance, a First Great Western HST approaches Platform 4.

Below:
Class 460: Clapham Junction August 2001
Gatwick Express Class 460 No 460005 approaches Platform 13, en route to Gatwick Airport. Its abbreviated identity, '05', is somewhat indistinct, the numerals being in white. In later years, it was with some relief that black numerals were adopted as standard. There are only eight eight-coach units in this class, Nos 460001-008.

Above:

Class 313 in service with Southern:
Brighton August 2010
Recently arrived, Southern Class 313/2 No 313207 is parked in the west carriage road at Brighton, between Platforms 2 and 3. At this time several units had already been repainted in Southern livery, and a programme of internal refitting had commenced. Units in service prior to refitting carried large pictures, advertising 'before and after' furnishings. The Class 313 units date from 1976-77, and were formerly in service with Silver Link and, subsequently, London Overground before being displaced by Class 378. Nineteen units were transferred, due for repainting, refitting and renumbering during 2010, as Nos 313201-217/219/220.

Right:

Class 442 in service with Gatwick Express:
Brighton March 2010
Class 442 No 442414 stands in Platform 7 on a return service to Victoria, at a time when the class was advancing its presence on such services. It displays the Gatwick Express livery, for which operation the class was primarily redeployed with Southern, following its extraordinary – perhaps incredible – withdrawal from service by South West Trains. Class 442 comprises 24 5-coach units, Nos 442401-424, delivered to the South Western division in 1988/89. For Gatwick Express and other services with Southern, the class was refitted internally and re-liveried, externally.

Above:

Class 465, as modified by Hitachi: Hither Green April 2011

No 465019 leaves on a service to Dartford, modification by Hitachi identified externally by the removal of skirting panels below the bodywork, a striking visual contrast. The first unit to be thus modified was 465/1 No 465181. 97 four-coach BREL Networkers, Nos 465001-050 and 465151-197, were delivered between 1991 and 1994. There are slight detail differences between the two batches. Classes 465/0 and 465/1 have three ventilator grilles above the windows, an external feature that distinguishes them from Classes 465/2, 465/9 and 466. In this picture, 465/0 No 465019 exhibits the latest style of door panels, with pale blue replacing yellow, but it carries neither grey nor black shading beneath the windows, a subsequent livery development.

Left:

Class 465/2 modified as Class 465/9: Canterbury West May 2005

No 465917 enters platform 1, forming a service to Victoria, via Ashford and Maidstone East. The train is framed by the impressive gantry signal box at the Ramsgate end of the station. The SER station had opened as Canterbury in 1846. Confusingly, the LCDR station, Canterbury East, also opened as Canterbury, 14 years later in 1860. Both stations acquired their present identities in 1899, following a 'working union' between the two companies in that year. Formerly Class 465/2 No 465217, the unit was refitted with 1st class seating and new panelling, one of the 34 four-coach Metro-Cammell units to have been thus modified as Class 465/9, Nos 465201-234 becoming Nos 465901-934. Metro-Cammell Classes 465/2 and 465/9 do not have a set of three ventilator grilles above the windows.

Bottom left:

Class 508 in service with Southeastern, previously Connex: Penshurst December 2008

During the final days of Class 508 operation in public service with Southeastern, No 508205 arrives from London Bridge on a service to Tunbridge Wells. The original station opened in 1842 but the present appointments are of more recent construction. Twelve units of this class, Nos 508201-212 were transferred to Connex South Eastern from Merseyrail, where they had been numbered 508101/105/106/107/109/113/116/119/121/129/132/133 respectively. Prior to being with Merseyrail in the early 1980s, they had started life with British Rail (Southern Region) from 1979, numbered 508001 etc., working suburban services on the South Western Division.

Above:
Ascot June 2000
An extra service for the local race meeting – Ascot Week - stands in Platform 3, formed by '4CEP' No 1565. Remodelled when the route was electrified in 1939, the station had opened originally in 1856 with the building of the line to Wokingham, there to join the SER line to Reading. The line from Ascot to Sturt Lane Junction was opened in 1878. Platform 1 has two platform faces, either side of a single track, with Platform 2 the outer face of the island platform, seen here to the right.

Below:
Ashford August 2000
Prior to the installation of 25kV wiring, Class 373 No 373019 leads a Eurostar formation into the International island Platform 3, Waterloo-bound.

Left:
Ashford September 2003
'4CEP' No 1594 stands in the new Platform 6, with the High Speed line to the left. 1594 exhibits the deplorable condition in which many units were to be found towards the end of their working lives. Internally, likewise, much was to be deplored, with upholstery often badly soiled and damaged, while lavatories could be found locked out of use. It was not unknown for some doors to be inoperable. The unit had recently come in from Margate.

Below:
Ash Vale June 2000
'4VEP' No 3468 comes over the junction at Ash Vale, forming a train from Waterloo to Alton. The line to the left is the link with Ascot, via Frimley and Camberley, which is single track from just beyond the junction to Frimley Junction, a distance of under two miles. Frimley Junction had, at one time, provided links with the up and down main lines between Woking and Basingstoke. The electrification scheme was extended from Virginia Water to Ash Vale in January 1939, to join the 1937 Woking-Alton scheme.

Above:

Aylesford May 2000

'4VEP' No 3587 arrives on a shuttle service from Maidstone West to Strood. Semaphore signals control the station, where the building features Caen Stone wall dressings. It is a tall, imposing building, sadly too tall for the camera to accommodate the chimneystack, taken from a position on the footbridge. The signal box is seen just beyond the 1856 station building.

Centre left:

Barnham September 2006

SWT Class 450 No 450110, the final unit from the initial batch, departs from Platform 2 on a service from Brighton to Basingstoke. SWT services east of Havant ceased from the December 2007 timetable. The station, opened in 1864, was known as Barnham Junction until 1929. Electrification came in 1938. The outer face of the island platform, here to the right, is principally the preserve of Bognor Regis traffic, though the main line west is accessible from this platform face.

Left:

Barnham May 1999

Having left the station, Phase II '4CIG' 1845 takes the curve towards Bognor Regis, with a shuttle service between the two stations. The substation and associated electrical structures at the junction are visible above the fencing.

Left:

Basingstoke August 2000
Substantial canopies at the station frame new Class 458 unit No 458012, identified only by the last four digits. The unit is on test, having come up from Bournemouth depot. The station opened in 1839 and the unit is using Platform 4; Platform 5, out of sight to the right, having Great Western associations, is used by services to Reading. The GWR reached Basingstoke in 1848, nine years after the LSWR extended its line from Winchfield (Shapley Heath) in 1839.

Centre left:

Bat & Ball September 2009
Class 319/4 No 319445 arrives with a train from Kentish Town to Sevenoaks. The station is situated on the original 1862 line from Sutton-at-Hone (Swanley), the branch to Maidstone East from Otford Junction opening twelve years later in 1874. Bat & Ball was the first LCDR station to serve Sevenoaks, the extension to Sevenoaks (Tubs Hill) coming in 1869. The building, though out of use and boarded up, retains much charm, with many interesting features. On the up side, the small canopy has a scalloped valance, an attractive, if unusual departure. No 319445 is liveried in the latest First Capital Connect style.

Below:

Bearsted August 2009
Class 375/9 No 375922 calls at the station, on a service from Ashford to Victoria, via Maidstone East. A neat, country station provides a welcome sight, and Bearsted is no exception. The LCDR canopies are typical, with attractive fretwork completing the design. The Southern Railway added a standard concrete footbridge, glimpsed in the background. The station had opened in 1884, as Bearsted & Thurnham, with the LCDR's advance towards Ashford.

Above:

Beckenham Hill May 2011
Class 465/0 No 465035 departs on a service from Sevenoaks to Victoria. The unit carries grey shading on the lower body panelling, a feature altered to Midnight Blue on later re-paints. The station opened with the Catford Loop in July 1892, a line that connects Nunhead with Shortlands. The original station building survives on the up platform, its canopy valance visible beneath the footbridge.

Left:

Beckenham Junction September 1999
The down side bay platform is used occasionally but was, for a while, used by a regular service, one that had come via New Beckenham. In this view, Class 465/1 No 465169, one of the second batch from BREL/ABB (465151-97), squeezes into the available space before returning to London. The goods yard once occupied space now taken by a supermarket. A typical LCDR canopy protects the platform. A station opened here originally as a terminus for the line from Lewisham. In 1925, electrification arrived, with through services between Victoria and Orpington.

Left:

Beckenham Junction June 2010
Class 465/0 No 465024 departs on a service
to Victoria via Herne Hill. It displays the very
latest livery for the class, following overhaul,
basically white but with pale blue doors;
these had previously been yellow. To the right
stands Class 455/8 No 455812 in the up side bay
platform, waiting to leave on a service to
London Bridge. On the left, in the down side
bay, stands the 1612 service to Charing Cross,
diagrammed to use the spur to New Beckenham.

Below:

Berwick June 2006
Class 377/4 No 377442 passes through, heading
an eight-coach train from Victoria to Ore. Only
the trailing unit will continue to Ore, the leading
unit being detached at Eastbourne. The signal
box controls not only semaphore signals at the
station but also the gates at a road crossing,
one that is quite busy.

Above:

Bexhill May 2000

Phase I '4CIG' No 1712 departs the station on a stopping service from Brighton to Ore. An imposing station building, complete with lantern roof, towers over two substantial sections of canopy, each sculpted with arced valance. At the time this picture was taken, the station had become sadly dilapidated. Indeed, broken glazing panels could be found in the footbridge area, fronting the stately building itself. Thankfully, a restoration scheme has rescued the situation.

Below:

Bexhill May 2011

Class 377/4 No 377423 arrives in Platform 1 on a Victoria service, to proceed via Lewes after reversal at Eastbourne. The restored, unashamedly grand station building at road level provides a backdrop of distinction. The structure dates from 1901, though the original station had opened with the line from Lewes to Bulverhythe (West Marina) in 1846.

Left:
Bexley December 2008
No 465241 is one of the last 16 of the original Metro-Cammell Class 465/2 delivery, the first 34 having been refitted to become Class 465/9, with provision for 1st class. The station is seen undergoing maintenance and repainting. Original wooden buildings and canopies enrich the station ambience, providing a welcome link with Loop Line history, dating back to 1866.

Centre left:
Bickley Junction September 1999
Class 465/0 No 465013, typically exhibiting a touch of graffiti, a prevalent curse at the time, approaches the junction from Bickley station with a train from Victoria to Orpington. The unit is one out-shopped in the Connex livery of blue white and yellow, the original Class 465 front-end design being evident.

Below:
Bincombe February 2004
Class 442 No 442412 takes the climb in its stride, as it approaches the site of former Upwey Wishing Well Halt, on a service from Weymouth to Waterloo, with the English Channel as a backdrop. The halt had closed in January 1957.

Top right:
Bishopstone August 2010
The branch line to Seaford having become a single line siding from Newhaven Harbour, the original down platform no longer serves any purpose. The up platform, with its rudimentary canopy, receives Class 313/2 No 313205, operating a stopping service from Seaford to Brighton. [Seaford station appears in the far distance and is identifiable from here by the lights on a train waiting to leave Seaford's only platform (curiously numbered '2').] The present station building dates from 1938 but its stylish, octagonal, road-level hall is now sadly a redundant relic of Southern Railway optimism.

Centre right:
Blackfriars September 1999
The terminus platforms at the station have since been demolished to accommodate a revised arrangement for through lines. In this scene, Class 465/0 No 465002, in Connex blue, white and yellow livery, waits in Platform 3, while Thameslink Class 319/4 No 319458 takes a pause from duty in Platform 2. Through lines to City Thameslink are on the extreme left of the picture. In the revised arrangement, through services from London Bridge do not have to cross the path of trains from Elephant & Castle.

Below:
Blackfriars September 1999
Class 319/3 No 319385, in Thameslink livery, enters Platform 5 on a service to Luton from the Wimbledon & Sutton loop. Piers that formerly carried LCDR tracks are incorporated, partially, in the rebuilding scheme for the station, to include public access from the South Bank. In the scheme, through lines transfer to the site of the former terminal platforms.

Above:
Blackfriars November 2001
The site of the original terminal platforms provides the track bed for the new through lines, the revised layout eliminating conflict that had existed between services from London Bridge and Elephant & Castle. Those serving London Bridge had previously to cross the path of those requiring the terminal platforms. In this view, Railtrack unit No 930008 is parked in

Platform 2. It comprises vehicles Nos 975596 and 975597, formerly Nos 10844 and 10987, respectively. These vehicles were formerly part of '4SUB' units Nos 4385 and 4124, respectively, rebuilt with EPB driving ends.

Below:
Blackfriars June 2010
Amidst the apparent chaos of alterations, Class 377/5 No 377503 arrives from City

Thameslink, on a service from Bedford to Brighton. By this time, the original terminal platforms and superstructure had been demolished, soon to make way for the through lines, with terminal platforms transferring to the west side to eliminate conflicting movements.

Above:
Blackheath February 2009
Class 376 No 376022 calls with a service from Dartford to Charing Cross. The station, opened in 1849 with additions dating from 1864, was an important point on the SER North Kent line. The well-maintained valance on the platform canopy contrasts with the television monitor structures of a later age, seen here to the right. Monitors were installed from the 1980s, allowing drivers to observe passengers leaving and boarding trains.

Left:
Bognor Regis May 2006
Class 377/1 No 377118 and Class 377/4 No 377416 stand in Platforms 2 and 3, respectively. The ironwork of the platform canopies is here seen to good effect, the stepped features in the valance contrasting with those found at Worthing.

Above:
Botley June 2009
On its approach to the station, Class 444 No 444041 passes the closed signal box, with a service from Waterloo to Portsmouth Harbour via Eastleigh. A station opened at Botley in 1842, with the line from Eastleigh to Gosport. The signal box, here out of use, had been retained to provide access to the stump of the Bishop's Waltham branch, serving the needs of aggregate traffic.

Below:
Bournemouth April 2003
'4CEP' No 1697 stands at the up platform, at the head of a stopping service to Waterloo. 1697 was one of a small sub-class of units fitted with BR Mk.6 bogies. This imposing 1885 station benefited greatly from a well-merited programme of refurbishment.

Above:

Bournemouth April 2003

Phase I '4CIG' 1714 stands in the bay platform, waiting to return to Victoria, via Haywards Heath. Not long afterwards, the service was curtailed to reverse at Southampton. The station was opened in 1885. The bucket of water and a brush, often a feature at platform ends, is provided for cleaning windscreens.

Centre left:

Branksome Junction July 2000

A well maintained, imposing signal box stood at the east end of Branksome station. It became redundant in December 2003 and was demolished in February 2004. This junction enables rolling stock, by reversal, to access Bournemouth depot, situated on the former main line to Bournemouth West. The line to the left, which the Class 442 unit is using, is from Bournemouth (formerly Central) station, while that to the right leads to the depot. In earlier times, the formation from Branksome Junction to Bournemouth West saw regular LMS traffic from the Somerset & Dorset. Branksome station opened in 1893.

Left:

Brighton November 2004

Phase II '4CIG' No 1805 stand in Platform 8 with a stopping train bound for Ore. The site of former Platforms 9 and 10, to the left of the unit, now provides access to a parking area. The imposing iron train shed, dating from 1882/3, had recently been repainted in blue, with decorative features picked out in contrasting colours. This replaced the previous scheme in brick red.

Left:

Brighton June 2001
Phase II '4CIG' No 1850 enters Platform 2 on a service from West Worthing. The former steam locomotive depot site is immediately behind the unit. Platform 3 is the only platform at Brighton with access to both the north and the west.

Bottom:

Brighton May 2003
Class 375/3 No 375333 is about to depart from Platform 6, at the head of a Victoria fast service. This unit eventually became Class 377/3 No 377323, when the couplings were modified. The first ten Class 375/3 units (375301-310) were allocated to Southeastern, where they remain.

Top right:

Brighton May 2003
Unusually, South West Trains '4CEP' No 1539 stands in Platform 2, awaiting departure on a service to Southampton, on an occasion when engineering work closed the main line to Basingstoke, where the train would normally have gone.

Bottom right:

Brighton June 2001
Thameslink Class 319/3 unit No 319375 stands alongside Connex Class 319/2 No 319215, the latter wearing an advertising livery. The units occupy Platforms 7 and 6, respectively. The advertisement celebrates 'Connex Days out'.

Above:
Brockenhurst October 2005
'3CIG' No 1497 waits in Platform 4, about to depart on a shuttle service to Lymington Pier.

Left:
Cannon Street June 2010
The imposing 120ft western tower offers a commanding presence at the country end of the terminus, the matching eastern tower providing pleasing architectural balance. A modern structure is now inserted between the towers where once there existed a large iron train shed. The station was opened in September 1866, with the towers a surviving feature of the original design. Class 465/0 No.465005 is about to leave on a Dartford service.

Top right:
Chatham September 2002
Metro-Cammell Class 465/2 No 465227 emerges from Fort Pitt tunnel to arrive at the station, while '4VEP' No 3472 waits in the up platform with a service to Victoria from Ramsgate. Rochester, on the other side of the tunnel, is only 44 chains distant.

Centre right:
Chessington North September 2009
The original 1939 structures are seen 70 years after their construction, the Chisarc canopies and lift shaft structure having stood the test of time. Had WWII not intervened to bring Southern Railway modernization to an abrupt halt, it was intended to extend the branch from Chessington South to Leatherhead, through what was later to be designated 'green belt' territory. Class 455/8 No 455854 (5854) stands in the up platform on a service to Waterloo.

Bottom right:
Clapham Junction August 1999
Class 73/2 No 73213 rounds the curve from Battersea Park on a Gatwick Express service. The viaduct connection to Victoria, taking the line over South Western tracks from Waterloo, was completed in 1860, replacing the original terminus at Battersea.

Left:
Clapham Junction August 2001
Class 458 No 458006 races Class 455/9 No 455904 (5904) into Platforms 6 and 11, respectively. 455904 wears a SWT advertising livery.

Centre left:
Clapham Junction September 2009
A wide view taken from the spacious footbridge finds Class 458 No 458021 (8021) arriving at Platform 6, heading an eight-coach train for Reading. The tracks in the foreground lead to the many storage sidings, situated in the space between Platforms 6 and 7.

Bottom:
Clapham Junction April 2007
Yet to be refurbished and out-shopped in SWT red livery, Class 455/8 No 455860 (5860) arrives in platform 11 on a through service to Guildford, via Epsom. A pigeon glides towards the camera, seen above the driver's door. The original SWT livery was basically the same as that for Network South East, with the addition of an orange band.

Top right:
Clapham Junction June 2009
London Midland's Class 350/1 350120 takes the Platform 16 fork at Falcon Junction; bound for Milton Keynes; it has come from East Croydon. Class 350 was used on these services while Class 377/2 units were temporarily on loan to First Capital Connect, the delivery of Class 377/5 having been delayed.

Bottom right:
Cosham December 2007
Class 377/1 No 377116 leaves the station en route from Southampton to Victoria. The station opened in 1848 as a joint venture by the LBSCR and the LSWR. The freight yard occupied land to the right in the picture.

Above:

Crystal Palace March 1999

The through lines to Sydenham had become reduced in importance over many years, during which time the grand station building became sadly dilapidated. Vegetation consumed the area between the platforms, where sidings had existed. In this view, Class 455/8 No 455841 (5841) awaits departure towards London Bridge. The West End and Crystal Palace Railway had inaugurated services from here in December 1856. In recent years, the building was restored and, most recently, vegetation has given way to a new platform, serving London Overground services to Dalston Junction.

Below:

Crystal Palace June 2010

With the new platform built and in service, Class 378/1 No. 378151 is about to depart on a service to Dalston Junction.

Above:

Dartford January 1998

Class 465/1 No 465197, the last of the BREL/ABB production series, stands in Platform 2, waiting to return to London. Dartford opened with the North Kent line in 1849 but subsequently became the merging point for all three suburban lines from London. The Dartford Loop arrived in 1866, followed by the Bexleyheath line to Slades Green (later renamed Slade Green) in 1895. The architecture seen here dates from the BR(SR) period.

Below:

Dover Priory June 1999

Priory station island Platform 3 hosts Class 365 No 365507 waiting to leave on a service to Victoria via Canterbury East. In Platform 1, '4VEP' No 3495 is on a service to Charing Cross via Ashford, having come from Margate. Priory station was opened by the LCDR in 1861 but the present structure dates from Southern Railway reconstruction.

Left:
Dover Priory June 1998
The southern approach to the station is through the 684-yard Dover Harbour tunnel. '4VEP' No 3511 bursts into the sunshine, having come from Charing Cross on a service to Margate. The sidings, glimpsed to the right, used to provide a resting place for steam locomotives, with the former motive power depot on the other side of the tunnel, about 67 chains distant.

Below:
East Croydon March 2010
In 'as delivered' condition, Class 377/5 No 377522 departs from Platform 2 on a service to Bedford from Brighton. It had yet to receive First Capital Connect decorative vinyls, unarguably a disfiguring addition (see the Haywards Heath picture for comparison), given the elegance and simplicity of design displayed here.

Top right:
East Croydon August 2009
Class 319/2 No 319218 arrives in Platform 3 on a First Capital Connect service to Brighton from the former Midland main line. Though still in Southern colours, the unit carries First Capital Connect branding on the body sides.

Above:

East Croydon March 2010
Recently reinstated to operate Gatwick Express services, Class 442 No 442421 leads a 10-coach formation through Platform 3, en route from Victoria to Gatwick Airport. Class 442 units were progressively repainted and refitted internally, during their early months of service on the Brighton main line.

Right:

East Grinstead March 2006
Class 377/1 No 377133 has just arrived at Platform 2 on a service from Victoria. Empty stock is parked in Platform 1. The original low level station had opened in 1882, while the long since closed high level station (for Three Bridges and Tunbridge Wells) had been connected to the low level line from Oxted at St. Margaret's Junction, to the north of this station. Electrification extended from Sanderstead in 1987.

Left:
Eastleigh March 2008
Class 377/3 No 377318 stands in Platform 3, in the process of reversal, on a service from Southampton to Brighton. The diagram required a Southern service to travel by this route to Fareham, in order that route knowledge might be maintained. The famous lime tree on the island platform survives as a significant link with decades past and was, at one time, host to a surrounding seat, forming a full circle.

Below:
Eastleigh April 2004
'4CEP' No 1612 leads an eight-coach rake into Platform 2, whilst operating from Waterloo to Portsmouth Harbour, via Basingstoke. The crude 1960s island platform building dates from the 1967 electrification scheme; it contrasts most unfavourably with the substantial iron footbridge, the latter evidently appearing to be in need of sensitive renovation.

Top right:
Eastleigh August 2006
'3CIG' No 1498 is reversing in Platform 2, having arrived from Bournemouth. Taking units to Fareham, thence to return via Netley, allowed wear on Lymington branch rolling stock to be equalized. 1498 wears a green livery, while its partner, No 1497, was out-shopped in blue-grey, this being authentically correct.

Above:
Eastleigh September 2005
On the 17th day of the month, a valedictory tour with Mk.I rolling stock travels fast through the station. Earlier in the day, the train had started from Ramsgate (dep. 0556), travelling via Dover, Maidstone East, Bromley South, Linford Street Junction, Nine Elms Junction, Waterloo (Platform 18), Sheepcote Lane curve, Kensington Olympia, Clapham Junction, Mitcham Junction, Dorking, Barnham, Southampton, Weymouth, Eastleigh, Woking, Staines, Twickenham, Clapham Junction, Factory Junction, Gillingham and Ramsgate (arr. 1943). Phase II '4CIG' 1866 leads the formation, with '4VEP' No 3445 and '4CEP' No 1698 behind; No 1698 was one of a small, re-bogied, sub-class of '4CEP' units.

Left:
Eastleigh January 2001
Appearing quite freshly outshopped, '4VEP' No 3558 passes the Works site on a semi-fast service from Waterloo to Bournemouth.
The down island platform, in the background, shows the famous lime tree in winter nakedness. The up platform, seen to the left, was originally an island, the site of former Platform 1 now given over to motor-traffic.

Left:
Egham April 2001
Class 455/8 No 455873 (5873), arrives at Platform 2 on a service from Waterloo to Weybridge. Egham station had been built in 1856 but is seen in this view rebuilt, thankfully not in the crude prefabrication style that characterized the 1960s.

Below:
Elephant & Castle May 2007
Class 319/3 No 319362 stands in Platform 2 on a service to Brighton. The unit wears the modified former Thameslink livery, with yellow band removed, replaced by white with First Capital Connect branding. In its original form as No 319162, this Class 319/3 unit had offered 1st class accommodation. The present station here was opened in 1863.

Left:
Erith January 1998
Class 465/0 No 465012, wearing the livery of Network South East, approaches the staggered up platform and is seen coming past the down platform and station building. The building is an imposing edifice, its canopy with original, decorated valance sheltering the platform. The station dates from the opening of the North Kent line in 1849.

Above:

Eynsford August 2009

Class 465/0 No 465004 drifts into the down platform on a service to Maidstone East. The unit displays to particularly good effect the revised front-end design, with the removal of grab rails and sloping upper edges to the yellow 'buffers'. The Swanley to Sevenoaks (Bat & Ball) line opened in 1862. The station building has great character, if denied a period platform canopy.

Below:

Falconwood February 2009

Class 376 No 376012, resting momentarily, basks in dappled winter sunshine, with a service from Dartford to Charing Cross. The station dates from as recently as 1936, though the Bexleyheath line had opened for business in 1895.

Right:

Falmer April 2000
'3COP' No 1403 arrives on an eastbound service from Brighton. The station dates from 1865, when the previous station, built in 1846 and situated on the other side of Falmer tunnel, was closed. The present buildings are of later construction, dating from the late 19th century. A signalling frame, now out of use, was installed on the platform, the glazed structure seen here alongside the train.

Below:

Farlington Junction September 2005
'4CEP' No 1698 leads the valedictory tour for Mk I rolling stock over the junction. The other units in the rake are '4VEP' No 3445 and Phase II '4CIG' No 1866. Nos 3445 and 1866 are in Connex yellow and white livery, while No 1698 displays quasi-NSE colours, its SWT livery having been modified (no orange) when it transferred to the Southeastern, for its final months in service. The roller blinds are from different periods, the 'tens' being in the original BR style, while the 'units' represent a style introduced not long before Mk.I rolling stock was withdrawn. The layout at the junction has since been revised, a crossover replacing the standard double track junction and diamond formation.

Left:

Farlington Junction November 2002
The unimaginative white livery, if thankfully used sparingly by Connex, nevertheless lends a distinctive appearance to Phase I '4CIG' No 1737, rounding the curve on the north side of the triangle at this point. The unit is bound for Victoria, having come from Bournemouth. Such services turned back at Southampton not long afterwards.

Centre left:

Farncombe February 2005
'4VEP' No. 3810, leased by Porterbrook, arrives at the head of a semi-fast service from Waterloo to Portsmouth & Southsea, according to the headcode '72'. However, as the train is 12-coach in length, either the code is expressing optimism or the train will terminate at Fratton, as the low level platforms at Portsmouth & Southsea could not accommodate such a rake. Farncombe station was opened as late as May 1897 and exhibits an interesting architectural style, post-dating the string of stations to the south, dating from 1859.

Below:

Faversham June 2009
Class 375/8 No 375814 arrives from Dover and is about to link up with a portion from Ramsgate, before continuing to Victoria. The former steam locomotive depot was situated in the fork of the junction, between the two routes to the east. A Class 465/9 unit stands in the up sidings alongside the line from Dover. The railway reached Faversham in 1858, electrification following 101 years later.

Left:
Faversham June 2009
Class 466 No 466003 emerges from the sidings to take up duty, augmenting a Class 465/9 unit in Platform 4, to form a six-coach stopping train to Victoria. Class 466 comprises 43 2-coach units, Nos 466001-043.

Centre left:
Faversham March 2010
Class 395 No 395010 rests in Platform 1, waiting to return to St. Pancras via Gravesend and HS1.

Bottom:
Folkestone Central August 2009
Class 375/8 No 375829 stands in Platform 1, now the south face of the only island platform in use. The abandoned former up island platform, seen in the background, is a depressing sight, with dereliction and weeds on display. The unit is about to return to Charing Cross from a station that was reconstructed at the time of electrification, in 1961/2. A seagull stands sentinel.

Right:
Fratton March 2007
During the 2007 period of re-signalling, services were curtailed west from Fratton station. In this scene, Class 377/4 No 377401, the first of its sub-class, awaits departure on a service to Victoria. It is leaving from Platform 2, an innovation facilitated by the new signalling arrangements, when Platform 3 also became bi-directional.

Bottom right:
Fratton March 2010
Class 444 No 444005 is about to leave Platform 1 on a service from Portsmouth Harbour to Waterloo. The new footbridge, opened only a few weeks earlier, here forms a backdrop. It is of a design to be found at other locations on the system, where lifts have been incorporated.

Above:

Gatwick April 1999
Ex-'2HAP' DMBSO (61298 from unit 6088), converted to be DMLV 9105, leads a return Gatwick Express service to Victoria. The Class 488/2 and Class 488/3 units display a modified livery below the waist for Airlines advertising. A Class 73 propels.

Below:

Gillingham June 2009
Class 395 No 395018 enters Platform 2, where it will pause before continuing west. It is on a training run from Ashford. The December 2009 timetable saw these units deployed on regular services, using the 25kV High Speed line to St. Pancras.

SOUTHERN EMUs SINCE PRIVATISATION **in colour**

Above:

Glynde April 2000

The roofed lattice footbridge is illustrated, as Phase I '4CIG' No. 1722 charges through, at speed, heading an eight-coach formation on a service bound for Victoria. The pink lamp-posts are a faded reminder of the NSE colour scheme.

Below:

Glynde April 2000

'3COP' No. 1409 arrives on a stopping service from Brighton, framed by the lattice footbridge. The period up side canopy survives, as do the down side station buildings, now happily in alternative commercial use, rather than abandoned to succumb to dereliction. These 19th-century buildings post-date the opening of the station in 1846.

Gravesend March 2010
Class 395 No 395014 pauses in Platform 1 with
a service from Faversham and is about to
continue to St. Pancras via Springhead Road
Junction and HS1, a route that became part of
the public timetable in December 2009. The
station opened with the North Kent line in 1849.
It had been preceded by a short-lived station
from 1845 until 1849, operated by the
Gravesend and Rochester Railway. The
buildings are restored and well maintained, the
entire station setting being one of gratifying
architectural merit.

Centre left:
Grove Park April 1999
Unique Phase II '4CIG' No 1812 stands in
branch Platform 1 with the shuttle service
to and from Bromley North. This unit was
experimentally fitted with central door locking,
a device not found in other such units at the
time. It therefore led a particularly lonely
existence, the Bromley North shuttle perhaps
being relegation for a former express unit.
The station opened in 1871.

Left:
Guildford March 2010
Class 455/9 No. 455903 (5903) leaves bay
Platform 1 on a service to Waterloo via the
1885 New Line, Bookham and Leatherhead.
No. 5903 is a member of the third and final
batch of Class 455 (5901-20), similar to the
first batch, Class 455/8, but with modified cab
ends, a style introduced with the second batch,
Class 455/7, in which one ex-Class 508 vehicle
per unit was incorporated.

Above:

Guildford October 2000

A 10-car rake of Class 442 stock arrives from the Woking direction on a fast service from Waterloo to Portsmouth Harbour. On the leading unit, jumper cable housings are exposed by the removal of the covers. In the immediate foreground is the line to Aldershot and Reading, while the 1885 New Line to Hinchley Wood is to the right.

Below:

Hampden Park July 2000

Phase I '4CIG' No 1734 departs on a service to Hastings and Ore. This will have departed Victoria as the trailing unit of an eight-coach train, the leading unit detached at Eastbourne. Hampden Park opened in 1888 as Willingdon, 39 years after the line itself into Eastbourne. The neat, compact little signal box is attractive, despite the absence of ornamentation.

Left:
Hampton Court September 2009
Class 455/8 No 455859 (5859), from the first batch, stands at the terminus. Restrained ornamental ironwork in the spandrels adds a pleasing touch to the operational island platform. The station opened in 1849, the substantial flyover at the junction on the main line following in 1915.

Below left:
Hampton Court September 2009
A view looking towards the buffers; Class 455/8 No 455859 (5859) is waiting to return to Waterloo. In this picture, the terminal structure is seen to extend to the left, embracing the disused island platform, an area since employed for bicycle storage. Sub-class 455/8 extends to 74 units; the first 46 are with Southern, while the final 28 are with SWT.

Below:
Haslemere August 2004
With not long to go before the demise of Mk.I rolling stock, '4CEP' (in formation) No 2311 arrives at the head of a stopping service from Waterloo to Portsmouth & Southsea. No 2311 had previously been numbered 2301, as a '4BEP' unit. However, the seven Greyhound '4BEP' units had had their buffet cars exchanged for non-buffet trailers from '4CEP' units, thus becoming in effect '4CEP' units, though retaining numbers in the '4BEP' series. Meanwhile, the '4CEP' donors became Nos 2321-27, following insertion of the buffet cars – but the buffets were out of use.

Left:

Haslemere February 2005
'4VEP' No 3540 is about to depart, at the head of a semi-fast service from Waterloo to Portsmouth & Southsea. It is true that '4VEP' rolling stock did, all too often, find its way on to main line fast services, the compensation being that the other unit in an eight-coach formation was invariably a '4CIG' or a '4CEP', offering 2+2 Standard class seating. The signal box at Haslemere stands on the down platform, its equipment, at this time, dating largely from the 1937 electrification of the route.

Centre left:

Hassocks August 2007
Class 319 unit Nos 319455 and 319370 pass in the station, each exhibiting the later Thameslink livery, here bearing First Capital Connect decals.

Below:

Hayes August 2002
Class 465/0 No 465042 stands in Platform 2 at this terminus station, waiting to return to Charing Cross at the head of an eight-coach formation. The end design of the unit is original, before measures were taken to prevent 'surfers' taking rides, standing on the 'white buffers', while grasping the grab rails. Photographs taken more recently demonstrate the resulting differences. The branch to Hayes was opened by the SER in 1882 but the station is of more recent Southern Railway design, following enemy attack during WWII. Television monitors, seen to the right, were installed in the 1980s, enabling drivers to observe passenger movements.

Above:

Herne Hill May 2007

Class 465/0 No 465029 arrives from Victoria. Front-end modifications to Class 465 are clearly seen in this portrait, yellow 'buffers' with sloping surfaces having replaced those with a horizontal upper surface. Grab rails have been removed. A distinguishing feature of Classes 465/0 and 465/1 is the set of three ventilator grilles above the windows, as seen here, in this respect contrasting with Metro-Cammell Class 465/2.

Centre right:

Hither Green May 2011

Taking the Dartford Loop line through Platform 6, Class 466 No 466015, leads a six-coach train on a service from Cannon Street to Dartford. Although the Loop line had opened in 1866, no station was provided at Hither Green until 1895. The unit carries one-piece grey shading on the lower body panels.

Right:

Horley September 2009

Class 460 Gatwick Express unit No 460002 runs through Platform 4, nearing the end of its journey to Gatwick from Victoria. The unit carries advertising livery, announcing Emirates Airlines (Australia), a variation on a theme echoed on other units. The station building is on the over-bridge in the background.

Left:
Horley September 2009
Class 319/4 No 319430 comes through Platform 3, the up fast line, en route from Brighton to London Bridge. This unit was the last to retain the silver and blue livery, surviving in this style as the only example over a very long period. Framed by the station canopy, the train catches the evening sunshine. A station opened here with the line in 1841 but was moved in 1905 when the lines were widened.

Below:
Hounslow September 2009
Class 450/5 No 450559 ('High Capacity' standing room) arrives at the down platform on a train for Windsor and Eton Riverside. The station building is a tall, imposing edifice, dating from 1850. The up platform canopy, being high, creates the illusion of the platform being narrow. Distinctive, arced brackets support the outer part of the canopy. The concrete footbridge, seen in the background, is an example of standard Southern Railway practice.

Left:
Hove May 2005
Class 377/1 No 377163 stands in Platform 1, the outer face of the island platform, while working a Southampton service from Victoria. The train had divided at Haywards Heath, the other portion making for Eastboune. The unit will have used the 1889 Cliftonville spur from Preston Park. The present station opened in 1865 as Cliftonville, becoming Hove in 1895. Platforms 1 and 2 are both reversible. The wooden-faced structure to the right of the unit contains the gentlemen's lavatory.

Centre left:
Hurst Green December 2002
Connex '4VEP' No 3518 arrives on a service from East Grinstead to Victoria. This view illustrates in close detail the features of a typical Southern Railway pre-fabricated concrete footbridge.

Bottom left:
Imperial Wharf March 2010
Class 377/2 No 377211 arrives on a service from Milton Keynes to East Croydon. The station is one of two recent openings, at this time, on the West London line, the other being at Shepherd's Bush. Some years earlier, the West London line had seen a new station opened at West Brompton. The building development, towering over the station in the background, is part of the Chelsea Harbour scheme, served by the station.

Top right:
Kensington Olympia June 2003
Class 73/1 Nos 73131 (leading) and 73136 (trailing) leave Platform 3 with the 1630 Willesden Railnet to Dover TPO. No 73131 wears the livery of EWS, while 73136 carries that for Main Line.

Bottom right:
King's Cross Thameslink June 2000
Class 319/4 No 319458 arrives from Bedford on a through service to Brighton. This station is now closed, having been replaced by the sub-surface station at St. Pancras International.

Above:

London Bridge May 2011
Class 465/2 No 465235 stands in platform 2 on
a service from Cannon Street to Dartford via
Greenwich. This unit, here outshopped with blue
doors, is one of the Metro-Cammell batch that
was not reformed with 1st class accommodation
as Class 465/9.

Left:

London Bridge February 2009
Class 377/4 No 377463 departs from high-level
Platform 5 on a service from Charing Cross,
via Redhill, to Tonbridge. Until the previous
December, Southeastern had operated from
the low level to Tunbridge Wells, via Redhill,
using mainly Class 508.

Above:
Lymington Pier October 2005
'3CIG' No 1497 comes round the bend from
Lymington Town station, while operating a
shuttle service from Brockenhurst. The unit is
one of two former '4CIG' units, reduced to three
vehicles, specifically for use on the branch. 1497
is in BR blue-grey livery. The branch had opened
to the Town station in 1860, the extension to the
Pier coming 24 years later, in 1884. The branch
is no more than a single line 'siding' from
Brockenhurst Junction, covering a distance of
4 miles and 70 chains from that point.

Centre left:
Lymington Town March 2007
The pleasingly substantial station building
survives and here receives green liveried '3CIG'
No 1498, travelling to Brockenhurst. This station
dates from 1860, though there had been a
temporary station at Lymington in 1858.

Left:
Maidstone East February 2000
'4VEP' No 3589 stands in the bay platform 3 and
is about to return to Victoria by the Herne Hill
route. The station opened in 1874, as a major
point on the LCDR extension from Otford
Junction to Ashford. The two through platforms
flank a central passing loop. All three tracks are
signalled for bidirectional running.

Top right:
Mitcham Eastfields March 2010
Class 455/8 No 455813 arrives at the station, one
recently opened at this time, on a service from
Epsom to Victoria. The platforms are staggered,
being on either side of a level crossing. South of
Streatham Junctions, the station is not far distant
from the site of erstwhile Eardley sidings.

Bottom right:
Motspur Park September 2009
Class 455/8 No 455871 (5871) is about to depart
from the island platform, en route to Guildford,
via Epsom. The station opened in 1925, when the
line from Raynes Park to Dorking was
electrified. It became a junction for the
Chessington South branch just over a decade
later, in 1938/9.

SOUTHERN EMUs SINCE PRIVATISATION in colour

Above:

Mottingham May 20201108

Class 465/0 No 465049 arrives at the country end of the station, en route to Dartford. The station opened as Eltham in 1866 but was renamed in 1927, a year after the 1926 electrification of lines to Dartford. The down side building is of 19th-century wooden construction but canopies are self-evidently of much later design. The unit combines grey shading on the lower body panels with pale blue doors, an intermediate livery.

Below:

New Cross Gate March 2010

Class 378/1 No 378147 arrives in Platform 5, the up slow line, on a staff training run from Crystal Palace, prior to the introduction of Class 378 into passenger services. Some interesting architectural features are to be seen at the station, with elderly buildings surviving in remarkably good condition; the wooden structures beneath the elegant canopy on Platforms 3 and 4 are of particular note. The station had opened in 1839 as New Cross on the London and Croydon railway, 'Gate' being added by the Southern Railway in 1923, to distinguish between the two stations in New Cross. The East London line connection dates from 1869.

Above:

Newhaven Harbour May 2011

Class 313/2 No 313215 arrives in the down platform on a stopping service from Brighton to Seaford. It is about to take the sharp curve to its left, en route to Bishopstone and Seaford. A station opened here in 1847 with the line from Southerham Junction to NewhavenWharf. The dilapidated station building survives, desperately in need of appreciative attention, given its association with the line's history. The terminus station that once served cross-channel shipping also survives. It is immediately behind the camera, its structure in such a perilous condition that passenger access is prohibited at the time of writing. The extension from Newhaven Harbour to Seaford was opened in 1864.

Below:

Norwood Junction December 2008

Class 508/2 No 508211 leaves Platform 4 on a service from London Bridge to Tunbridge Wells, via Redhill. This service was about to be withdrawn by Southeastern, to be replaced by a Southern service to Tonbridge. Commencing with the new timetable, Class 508 was taken out of service by Southeastern. The present station was opened by the LBSCR in June 1859. Original canopies have been replaced on island Platforms 4 and 5 but survive elsewhere, a corner of that to Platform 3 being just visible. Platforms 1 and 2 serve the same track, being either side of a single line; other electrified examples of this practice are to be found at Ascot and Guildford.

Left:
Otford August 2009
Class 465/1 No 465188 arrives in the down platform on a service to Maidstone East. The Maidstone line, dating from 1874, diverges east at Otford Junction, where it leaves the original 1862 line from Swanley to Sevenoaks (Bat & Ball). The station building on the up side is of substantial size; thankfully, it survives, enjoying a new life in alternative use. A standard LCDR canopy graces the up side platform. No 465188 had, by this time, been rebuilt with Hitachi equipment, conspicuously altering the appearance below the coach body.

Below:
Paddock Wood September 2002
Class 508/2 No 508203 arrives in the down platform, en route to Maidstone West; it had come from Gatwick Airport, reversing at Redhill. Many units suffered graffiti attacks at this time yet there seemed little determination by operating companies to expunge the evidence within hours. In allowing rolling stock to continue in service thus disfigured, vandals were effectively encouraged in their crimes.

Above:
Parkstone July 2000
Class 442 No 442416 races down the hill from Branksome to Poole. Opened in 1874, the station building on the up side contrasts with minimal protection offered on the down side. The canopy clings to the station building, somewhat after the style of a verandah.

Below:
Penge East May 2007
Class 373 No 373012 moves cautiously towards Penge tunnel on a service from Gare du Nord to Waterloo. The units were in their last few months of third rail operation into Waterloo, before moving to the 25kV High Speed line to St.Pancras. The LCDR station opened in 1863; a contemporary station house on the up side provides an interesting juxtaposition with the Eurostar.

Above:
Penge East May 2007
Class 465/2 No 465249 arrives on a stopping service to Orpington. This unit is one of the last 16 members of the sub-class, none of which underwent conversion to Class 465/9. Nos 465201-234 became 465901-934, when provision was made for 1st class.

Centre left:
Petts Wood Junction April 1999
Phase II '4CIG' No 1879 heads an eight-coach service to Hastings over the junction with the Tonbridge Loop, seen in the bottom left of the picture. The loop links the LCDR at Bickley Junction with the SER at this point and was used regularly by Eurostar. No 1879 carries Network South East livery but the second unit is in the 'white' livery.

Left:
Pevensey & Westham May 2000
The down side station building and canopy are joined by an attractive signal box, which controls the road crossing. Semaphore signalling adds to the period nature of the location. Phase I '4CIG' No. 1708 arrives on a service from Victoria to Ore; it will have formed the rear unit of the train that left London, the other unit (or units) deposited at Eastbourne.

Top right:
Polhill September 2003
On the rise to Polhill tunnel from Dunton Green, '4VEP' No 3804 sweeps round the bend on a service from Ashford to Charing Cross. The 12 38xx series '4VEP' units were leased by Porterbrook, the first eight of the sub-class being with Southeastern.

Right:
Poole April 2003
Greyhound '4CIG' No 1314 arrives at the up platform, having just crossed from the down main line, on a stopping service from Waterloo. Before returning to London, it visited the up siding. The line from Bournemouth to Poole opened in 1874.

Left:
Poole April 2003
A Class 442 from Weymouth enters the up platform, en route to Waterloo. The former goods yard on the up side, seen to the right, contains an electrified reversing loop and siding. The signal box is seen opposite, on the down side.

Centre left:
Portcreek Junction May 1998
Class 442 No 442418 passes through on a service from Waterloo to Portsmouth Harbour. The unit is in the original 1988 livery of Network South East, bands of white, red and blue, but with small SWT stickers attached centrally beneath the windows. Sharing of these excellent units between Bournemouth and Portsmouth brought comfort and elegance to the 1859 Direct route, an inspired move at the time by Network South East, yet one eventually to be withdrawn by SWT.

Bottom:
Portsmouth July 1997
Phase II '4CIG' No 1835 passes over the site of the former road crossing at Copnor, north of Fratton, where the proposal for a station never materialized. The former crossing keeper's house can be glimpsed through the bare trees on the left. The train, bound for Portsmouth Harbour, has come from Victoria, a service recently taken over by the new franchisee, Connex South Central. The unit is in the livery of Network South East.

Top right:
Portsmouth Harbour May 2007
Class 444 No 444028 arrives at the terminus and is entering Platform 3, having come from Waterloo on a fast service. Brand new signal gantries are in place, transforming the appearance of the approach. At this time, the new signalling system was causing immense problems and, as evidenced here, the new signals had yet to be commissioned.

Above:

Portsmouth Harbour May 2004

Greyhound '4CIG' No 1308 heads a Waterloo bound fast service from Platform 3. Platform 2 alongside is not served by track, presumably easing the weight on the supporting columns that date from the station opening in 1876. *Greyhound* units formed a sub-class of '4CIG' units, Nos 1301-22/92-99, incorporating electrical modification to improve the maximum speed. *H.M.S. Warrior*, to the left, and *H.M.S. Victory* provide an imposing backdrop.

Right:
Purley September 2003
'4VEP' No 3437 departs on a stopping train to Horsham from Platform 4. In the background is Platform 6, from which trains leave for Tattemham Corner and Caterham. Purley opened as Godstone Road in 1841, becoming Purley in 1888. Reconstruction in 1899 followed years of inter-company rivalry.

Below:
Putney August 2003
Class 455/7 No 455709 (5709) arrives on a Kingston circular, via Richmond, to Waterloo. The unit still wears the livery of Network South East, many years after the founding of SWT. The station opened in 1846, rebuilding following in 1886.

Above:

Rainham June 2009

Class 375/6 No 375806 departs from Platform 2 on a service from Victoria to Ramsgate and Dover. The imposing signal box structure, a bold statement of 20th century modernism, dominates the scene. The original station had been opened in 1858 but the buildings were demolished in 1972, when the present accommodation was provided.

Below:

Ramsgate November 2004

A fine signal box stands between the maintenance depot and the station. In Platform 4, Class 375/8 No 375802 waits to leave on a service to Charing Cross, via Canterbury West and Tonbridge. The station dates from major changes that took place in 1926, when the line from Margate was opened.

Above:

Redbridge Junction March 2001

Phase II '4CIG' No 1855, en route from Bournemouth to Victoria via Haywards Heath, crosses the junction where the line from Salisbury meets that from Bournemouth. The unit carries Connex livery, the yellow roof strip indicating 1st class accommodation. The main line from Blechynden (later replaced by Southampton West/Central) to Brockenhurst opened in 1847, the link from Redbridge Junction to Romsey following in 1865.

Below:

St. Denys April 2003

Phase II 4CIG No 1862, attired in Southern livery, speeds past the former goods yard at Bevois Park, on a service from Victoria to Southampton. A loop is retained on the up side, visible in the undergrowth. Southern livery in the style illustrated lasted so briefly, all such units being withdrawn within two years.

Above:
St. Margaret's September 2009
Class 455/8 No 455874 (5874), the last member of the first batch, departs with a 'Kingston circular' service. The station was opened in 1876. It features an island platform in the up direction. A more recent extension to the platform is evident in this view. The business part of the station is situated on the footbridge, seen in the background.

Left:
St. Mary Cray Junction April 1999
'4CEP' No 1576 is crossing to the down Chatham fast line, which uses Platform 2 at Swanley. Though the front end of the unit is reasonably clean, the Network South East livery is somewhat faded. The code '64' was originally used for Victoria – Catford – Sittingbourne – Sheerness; later reference suggests Victoria – Bat & Ball – Deal – Margate but its use here is uncertain. In the background is the single line connection from Chislehurst, the Reversible Chatham Loop; in the up direction, a burrowing junction connects with Chislehurst. The loops date from 1904, five years after a working arrangement between the LCDR and the SER had been established.

Left:
St. Mary Cray Junction April 1999
Class 92 No 92018 *'Stendhal'* heads for
Wembley, having come from Dollands Moor
with traffic from the continent of Europe.

Bottom:
St. Mary Cray Junction April 1999
Class 365 No 365515, in Connex livery, passes
through on the up Chatham slow line with an
eight-coach train bound for Victoria.

Right:
St. Mary Cray Junction April 1999
Class 365 Express Networker No 365512 takes
the sylvan spur to Chislehurst from the junction.
It is shortly to dive under the SER main line,
before travelling over a short section of the
down slow line from Bickley Junction to
Petts Wood Junction at Hawkwood Junction.
Following this manoeuvre, it will fork right, to
cross the LCDR main line, before merging with
the SER up fast line at Chislehurst Junction.
No 365512 is one of a batch of 16 express units
delivered in 1994/5. About a decade after
delivery, these units were transferred to operate
out of King's Cross, there to join the rest of the
class, operating in 25kV mode.

Bottom right:
St. Pancras International April 2008
Class 319/0 No 319001, now in First Capital
Connect livery, arrives at the recently opened
sub-surface station, with a service from
Brighton to Bedford. The station replaced that
at King's Cross Thameslink in December 2007.

SOUTHERN EMUs SINCE PRIVATISATION in colour

Left:
Selhurst September 2009
Class 455/8 No 455802 arrives in Platform 2 on a service from Caterham to Victoria. The roofs of the extensive servicing depot at Selhurst appear to the left in this view. The fast lines are to the right of the island platform. The station opened for business in 1865.

Below:
Selhurst July 2004
The eastern approach to the station is complicated. In this view, Class 319/0 No 319006 is rounding the curve from the direction of Norwood Junction on an empty stock working. Selhurst maintenance depot is to the left, out of view. The double track section to the right takes the slow lines to East Croydon, with a turnout to the far right for West Croydon. The lines from the near right, behind the colour light signal, allow traffic to pass between fast and slow lines at this point, Selhurst Junction.

Above:
Sevenoaks September 2009
Class 375/3 No 375304 leads a seven-coach
formation into Platform 3 on a train bound for
Dover and Ramsgate, with division at Ashford.
The station was modernized by BR(SR) and is
not unattractive as a functional design. A BR
symbol, redolent of the 1960s and mounted
above the building, makes a strong statement.
Sevenoaks, originally subtitled Tubs Hill,
opened in 1868 with the completion of the
cut-off; this offered a shorter route to Tonbridge
from London, avoiding Redhill.

Centre left:
Sevenoaks September 2009
Former Southern Class 319/2 No 319215 arrives
in Platform 4 with a train from Kentish Town.
The unit had by this time been transferred to
First Capital Connect; while Southern identity
had been removed, that for FCC had yet to be
applied. The word 'Bedford' is a premature
statement, though the train was due to return
to that destination a few minutes later.

Left:
Shawford February 2009
Class 450 No 450036 enters the station on a
stopping service from Waterloo to Poole.
The station opened in 1882; the link to the GWR
at Winchester Chesil, via a junction to the north,
came nine years later.

Above:
Sheerness-on-Sea February 2006
Class 508/2 No 508204 waits in the station with a shuttle service to Sittingbourne. Evidence of a centre track survives, a legacy from steam operation. The canopies are uncharacteristically neither horizontal nor of great depth. The present station is a 1922 replacement for the 1883 station, which had been on a different site.

Below:
Sittingbourne June 2009
Refitted Metro-Cammell Class 465/9 No 465907 departs on a stopping service to Faversham. The station had opened in 1858 and was, during a later period, known as Sittingbourne & Milton Regis. The building on the up side is probably contemporary with the line's opening, in part, at least. The branch to Sheerness-on-Sea uses the outer face of the island platform.

Top right:
Smitham May 2011
On the final day when the station carried this identity, the 21st of the month, Class 455/8 No 455813 arrives on a service from London Bridge to Tattenham Corner. The branch opened in three stages under the SER, at a time when the Joint Committee with the LCDR was incubating (1899): Purley to Kingswood (November 1897), Kingswood to Tadworth (July 1900) and Tadworth to Tattenham Corner (June 1901).

Smitham station, since rebuilt, was opened in January 1904 and renamed Coulsdon Town on 22 May 2011.

Right:
Snodland May 2000
Class 508/2 No 508209 drifts past the signal box, controlling the road crossing, before entering the up platform. The unit is operating a service from Maidstone West to Gillingham; after reversal at Strood, it will continue eastwards. The SER station opened with the line from Strood in 1856, providing a signal box and station building that are undeniably attractive.

Above:
South Croydon March 2010
Class 460 No 460004 accelerates through
Platform 2 on a Victoria to Gatwick service,
an operation at this time shared with Class 442.
The station, which the train is seen approaching,
was opened in 1865.

Centre left:
South Croydon March 2010
Class 456 No 456023 leaves Platform 3,
the up slow line, on a service from Caterham to
London Bridge. The traditional station building
and canopies form a backdrop to the scene,
with neatly clipped bushes adding decoration.

Bottom left:
Streatham Common September 2009
Class 456 No 456009, in Southern livery,
departs on a service from West Croydon to
London Bridge. The station opened in 1862
and is, like other suburban stations on the route,
build to a generous design. A fine brick building,
spacious platforms and extensive canopies
are a statement of confidence.

SOUTHERN EMUs SINCE PRIVATISATION in colour

Left:

Streatham Common September 2009
Class 455/8 No 455818 arrives on a service from London Bridge to West Croydon. When the former Central Division Class 455 units were eventually refurbished by Southern, their end gangways were removed with the opening sealed, as seen in this view.

Below:

Strood September 2002
Class 465/2 No 465227 comes round the sharp curve from Strood tunnel, bringing an eight-coach train into the station. It is bound for Gillingham. The station opened with the coming of the line from Gravesend in 1847. The line to Maidstone West followed in 1856. The link to Rochester and Chatham suffered the ravages of railway politics between the SER and LCDR, so the SER finally built its own line to Chatham Central, via Rochester Common in 1891/2, a line that closed in 1911. However, although the LCDR had built its own link to Strood from Rochester in 1858, it was not until the rival companies came together in 1899 that the situation was resolved, leading to an arrangement similar to that to be found today. Electrification to Gillingham and Maidstone West, via Strood, was inaugurated in 1939.

Above:

Swaythling August 2001

Class 442 No 442419 passes through, bound for Weymouth. In this view, jumper cable housing covers have been removed, a practice that was followed only intermittently in later years. The station here dates from 1883.

Below:

Three Bridges August 2003

Wearing Southern livery, Phase II '4CIG' 1857 leaves Platform 3 on a service to Bognor Regis. On the other side of Platform 5, seen here in the distance, was the bay used by steam push-pull services to East Grinstead.

Above:

Three Bridges August 2003
A rake of empty coaching stock, headed by
'4VEP' No 3529, clatters across the junction
with the 1848 Horsham branch. An electrical
sub-station stands in the junction fork,
behind which are engineering sidings,
formerly the site of the steam locomotive depot.

Left:

Tonbridge September 2003
In original Connex branding, Class 375/6
No 375606 stands in Platform 2 and is about to
depart for Charing Cross. The SER had reached
Tonbridge (originally Tunbridge) in 1842, via
the Redhill route, the Sevenoaks cut-off coming
26 years later. The present station dates from
Southern Railway rebuilding and exhibits the
clean lines that so characterized the company.

Above:

Tonbridge December 2008

Class 377/4 No 377469 rounds the curve from High Brooms on a through service from Tunbridge Wells to Horsham. This operation ceased from December 2008, when Southeastern relinquished services via Redhill to London Bridge. Southern then took over Tonbridge-Redhill duties, offering a through service to Charing Cross.

Below:

Tunbridge Wells April 2006

Class 377/4 No 377464 stands in Platform 1 and is about to return to Horsham on a through service, with reversal at Redhill. The station opened in November 1846, following completion of the tunnel; prior to this, a temporary station at Jackson Springs had served its purpose from September 1845. The attractive valance to the station canopies survives. Electrification came in 1986.

Above:
Upwey August 2005
Class 442 No 442405 arrives to collect passengers, on a service from Weymouth to Waterloo. On the former G.W.R. line from Swindon to Weymouth (mileages are from Paddington), the present station is no more than basic. The original station, sited nearby, carried the name Upwey and Broadwey.

Right:
Victoria March 2010
Platforms 13 and 14 are dedicated to Gatwick Express services. In this view, Class 460 No 460008 waits to leave from Platform 13 on a non-stop service to Gatwick Airport. The 'illuminated gloom' at Victoria replaced the once elegant iron and glass train shed of 1908. The station was rebuilt to serve the needs of commercial enterprise during the early 1980s, when a concrete raft was erected, which now covers Platforms 9 to 19.

Left:

Virginia Water April 2001
During a period of engineering work on the main line, Class 442 No 442404, with exposed jumper cables, leads a 10-coach rake round the sharp curve through Platform 3. It is en route to Waterloo, having come from Bournemouth and Weymouth. The line to this point opened in 1856. Electrification between Staines and Weybridge took effect from 1937, with that to Ash Vale and Reading following in 1939.

Below:

Virginia Water April 2001
Class 455/8 No 455873 (5873) takes the Weybridge route at the junction, on a service from Staines. The earlier lattice footbridge has been updated, with more recent steps, handrails and lighting.

Above right:

Wandsworth Common April 2003
Class 73 No 73201 runs through the cutting on the approach to the station with a Gatwick Express service. The train comprises five coaches and a Class 489 DMLV, the latter formerly a '2HAP' DMBSO. All were converted in 1983/4, the formation here containing a two-vehicle Class 488/2 and a three-vehicle Class 488/3, coaching stock dating originally from 1973/4.

Below:

Wandsworth Common July 2009
London Midland's Class 350/1 No 350118
calls at Platform 1 on a service from Milton
Keynes to East Croydon, during the period
when Southern loaned Class 377/2 units to
First Capital Connect, as a consequence of
the delayed delivery of Class 377/5 units.
The station building here is the second to bear
the title and dates from 1869. The first station,
differently positioned, had been opened in 1856
for the West End of London and Crystal Palace
Railway.

Right:

Wandsworth Road July 2009
Class 377/1 No 377132 arrives at the station to
operate the one-train-a-day obligatory service
to Kensington Olympia, fulfilling the need for
a passenger service to be provided over a route
from which a former inter-regional service had
been withdrawn. The unit had travelled as empty
stock from Streatham Hill depot.

Above:

Wandsworth Town August 2003
Class 455/8 No 455865 (5865) stands in
Platform 4 on a Hounslow loop service to
Waterloo. This unit is a member of the first
batch. The station opened in 1846, as a point on
the Richmond railway. Rebuilt and widened in
1903, the suffix 'Town' had already been added
in 1886. Attractive LSWR lettering survives
in ornamental relief on the station.

Below:

Wareham May 2010
Class 444 No 444036 arrives to take passengers
on the journey towards Waterloo. The first
station at Wareham, opened in 1847, was to the
east of the crossing. Business transferred to the
present 1886 station just after the branch to
Swanage opened in 1885. Attractive, original
architectural features survive, valance and
decorative ironwork here framing the arrival
of the Class 444 unit.

Top right:

Wareham May 2010
Class 444 No 444011 is on the point of leaving
for Weymouth, having come from Waterloo.
The down bay platform, to the right, was, at one
time, the departure point for push-pull services
to Swanage.

Bottom right:

Warnham April 1999
'4VEP' No 3479 stands at the down platform
on a stopping service to Horsham, upon which
route '4SUB' units once operated. The building
probably dates from 1867, when the line opened,
but no longer serves railway needs.

Above:

Wateringbury June 2000
A trailing view of '3CEP' No 1106, as it moves away towards Maidstone West. The station buildings offer much to attract the eye, with an exuberance of decoration though, regrettably at this time, ground level windows are boarded up. It is not always convenient to photograph trains coming towards the camera, the preferred aspect, this being a case in point, with restrictions to the right.1106 had started life as '4CEP' No 7141 over four decades earlier. While the line between Maidstone West and Paddock Wood dates from 1844, the building here is probably of later construction, perhaps dating from the opening of the northern section from Maidstone West to Strood in 1856.

Left:

West Malling August 2009
Refitted with 1st class accommodation, Class 465/9 No 465924 calls for custom, en route to Victoria, having come from Ashford. The station is one of some distinction, boasting a fine building on the up side, complete with a LCDR canopy protecting part of the platform. The station was opened in 1874 but some reconstruction followed in 1888. The line to Maidstone East had been electrified in 1939.

Left:

West St. Leonards May 2000
Phase II '4CIG' No 1839 brings an eight-coach Charing Cross to Hastings train round the sharp curve into the station. The line from Tonbridge to Hastings was completed in 1852, when the section between Battle and Bopeep Junction opened. However, the station at West St. Leonards did not open until 1887.

Centre left:

West St. Leonards May 2000
Bopeep Junction is immediately to the south of the station at West St. Leonards, where the LBSCR line from Eastbourne joins, that company having reached Bulverhythe (West Marina) in 1846, six years before the opening of the SER line. Phase II '4CIG' No 1842 comes round from Bopeep tunnel, past the signal box, on a service to Charing Cross from Hastings. Electrification of the line from Tonbridge to Bopeep Junction was achieved in 1986, when the Hastings Diesels were retired. The junction presents a rather cluttered appearance, with more recent infrastructure abutting a well-maintained signal box.

Below:

Weymouth May 2004
'4CEP' No 2316 stands at the buffers on Platform 3 and is about to return to Waterloo. 2306 had been renumbered as 2316 when its buffet car was swapped with a non-buffet trailer from a '4CEP'. This was done to increase the seating capacity in units upgraded to *Greyhound* status, full buffet facilities deemed no longer necessary. The '4CEP' that received the buffet coach from 2306 was renumbered 2326. As 2306, the unit seen here had been upgraded to operate with Portsmouth Direct-line '4CIG' units during the 1980s.

Above:
Whitstable June 2009
Class 375/6 No 375628 calls at the station with the Ramsgate portion of a train from Victoria, the train having divided at Faversham.
The LCDR station was opened in 1860. Rebuilding took place in 1914/15, bequeathing to present users a most attractive example of the company's idiosyncratic architecture. LCDR deep canopies grace both platforms but, unlike many earlier versions, a change in height of the pierced valance offers an attractive variation. The station had formerly carried the name Whitstable & Tankerton.

Below:
Winchfield September 2000
'4CEP' units, exiles from Kent, pass in the station. No 1578 speeds along the down fast on a semi-fast service, while a classmate leaves the up platform on a stopping train to Waterloo.

SOUTHERN EMUs SINCE PRIVATISATION in colour

Above:

Winchfield July 2003

Class 442 No 442409 heads a 10-coach rake through the station on the up through line, with a service from Bournemouth and Weymouth, bound for Waterloo. The station canopies exemplify economy of design by the LSWR, given the absence of any form of decoration to the finish. Winchfield was, at one time, a temporary terminus on the LSWR main line, opening in 1838 as Shapley Heath. The extension to Basingstoke followed in 1839. Quadrupling to Worting Junction was completed in 1909, with electrification coming in 1967.

Left:

Woking April 2000

The new Platform 3, a London end extension to the island platform, was inserted to receive trains terminating at the station. An up bay had, in former times, existed on the north side of Platform 1. '4VEP' No 3402 is waiting to depart on a stopping service to Waterloo. This unit was the second of the original batch of 20 units (7701-20), delivered in 1967 for the newly electrified services to Bournemouth.

Left:
Woolwich Arsenal January 1998
Class 465/1 No 465193 stands in the down platform, on a working from Charing Cross to Gravesend. The rotunda that came with the street-level station rebuilding is seen above the angled canopy. The red, blue and white flash on the cab is a legacy from Network South East. Woolwich Arsenal opened with the North Kent line in 1849.

Below:
Yalding May 2000
'3CEP' No 1111 arrives on a service from Maidstone West to Tonbridge and London Bridge via Rehill. The station opened in 1844 with the branch from Paddock Wood to Maidstone West. No 1111 had started life as '4CEP' No 7128.